UP NEXT)))

SPORTS ZONE SPECIAL REPORT

:02

FEATURE PRESENTATION:

:04

AVALANCHE FREESTYLE

FOLLOWED BY:

:50 **SPORTS ZONE POSTGAME RECAP**

:51 **SPORTS ZONE POSTGAME EXTRA**

:52 **SI KIDS INFO CENTRE**

SPORTS ZONE
SPECIAL REPORT

SNO
SNOWBOARDING

PNT
PAINTBALL

FBL
FOOTBALL

BSL
BASEBALL

BBL
BASKETBALL

HKY

TOP-RANKED TONY JAY IS EARLY FAVOURITE TO WIN SILVER FALLS TOURNAMENT

TONY JAY

STATS:
AGE: 15
EVENT: FREESTYLE

BIO: Tony's father, Calvin Jay, is the owner of Silver Falls Ski Resort. Calvin bought his son the best gear money can buy, and Tony's skills are incredible. In fact, the only shredder who has a shot at taking down Tony is Jack Hewlitt. There's just one problem — Jack can't afford to enter the competition, meaning that Tony will probably take home first place — and the famous Aurora-X snowboard!

UP NEXT: AVALANCHE FREESTYLE

JACK HEWLITT

AGE: 15
EVENT: FREESTYLE

BIO: Jack is a gifted shredder despite having to use a shabby board and well-worn bindings. Although his equipment is nowhere near top-notch, his skills are second to none, and he'll give Tony Jay a run for his money if he can find a way to enter the tournament...

DWAYNE KENT

AGE: 15
BIO: Dwayne is one of Tony Jay's many friends. Like Janice and Kevin, Dwayne spends a lot of time at the Jay family's mansion.

DWAYNE

CALVIN JAY

AGE: 43
BIO: Tony's father is a wealthy businessman who made a fortune in the music business. Now, he owns and runs the Silver Falls Ski Resort.

CALVIN

MARC HEWLITT

AGE: 47
BIO: Jack's father is a maintenance worker at Silver Falls Ski Resort. He does not make much money, but he loves his job – and his son.

MARC

PRESENTS

A PRODUCTION OF

raintree

a Capstone company — publishers for children

written by Scott Ciencin
illustrated by Aburtov
inked by Andres Esparza
coloured by Fares Maese

designed and directed by Bob Lentz
edited by Sean Tulien
creative direction by Heather Kindseth
editorial direction by Michael Dahl

Raintree is an imprint of Capstone Global Library, a company incorporated in England and Wales having its registered office at 264 Banbury Road, Oxford, OX2 7DY – Registered company number: 6695582

www.raintree.co.uk
myorders@raintree.co.uk

ISBN: 978 1 4747 7160 3
22 21 20 19 18
10 9 8 7 6 5 4 3 2 1

British Library Cataloguing in Publication Data
A full catalogue record for this book is available from the British Library.

Originated by Capstone Global Library Ltd
Printed and bound in India

This is the Silver Falls Ski Resort. My dad owns it.

A week from now, the resort will host the second annual Silver Falls Snowboarding Competition at our superpipe.

Up for grabs is the Aurora-X, the best board on the market – and I plan on taking first place.

Who am I? My name is Tony Jay ...

11

It's a shame that board's going to the best shredder who can **afford** to enter the competition . . .

. . . And not the best shredder at Silver Falls.

You're right. A victory wouldn't matter if I didn't beat the best.

So what do you have in mind, Jack?

Moments later . . .

I'm glad to hear that, son.

Jack doesn't seem like the type to take what's not his.

And Dad . . . Jack just saved my life, too.

Did he now? In that case . . .

. . . I'd like to sponsor you for the competition next week, Jack.

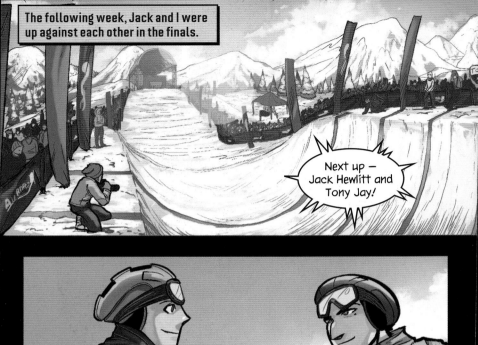

The following week, Jack and I were up against each other in the finals.

Next up — Jack Hewlitt and Tony Jay!

Are you ready to see who's the best, bro?

You know it!

Some other kid ended up winning the Aurora-X...

wHIRSHH!

wHIRSH!

SPORTS ZONE

POSTGAME RECAP

SNO
SNOWBOARDING

PNT
PAINTBALL

FBL
FOOTBALL

BSL
BASEBALL

BBL
BASKETBALL

HKY

BITTER RIVALS BECOME FAST FRIENDS AFTER OUTRUNNING AVALANCHE TOGETHER

BY THE NUMBERS

FREESTYLE EVENT FINAL SCORES:
TONY JAY: 9.6
JACK HEWLITT: 9.6
TY TAGGART: 9.7

STORY: An avalanche interrupted a freestyle duel between Jack Hewlitt and Tony Jay this weekend. The two teens were competing for the Aurora-X under the assumption that Tony Jay would later win it in the tournament. The unexpected event didn't faze the two teens – they simply shredded their way down the mountain with the deadly maelstrom of snow and ice nipping at their bindings.

UP NEXT: SI KIDS INFO CENTRE

Snowboarding fans got a real treat today when Tony Jay faced off against Jack Hewlitt in the Silver Falls Freestyle Tournament. Let's go into the stands and ask some fans for their opinions on the day's events...

DISCUSSION QUESTION 1

Tony Jay and Jack Hewlitt are total opposites in some ways. Do you think people who are very different can become good friends? Why or why not?

DISCUSSION QUESTION 2

Who do you like better – Tony Jay or Jack Hewlitt? What things do you like and dislike about each teen? Discuss your answers.

WRITING PROMPT 1

Imagine that you've won a snowboarding tournament, and your reward is a custom-built board! Name your new board, and write a few paragraphs about it. Then, draw a picture of your personalized reward.

WRITING PROMPT 2

Both Tony and Jack behave like heroes at certain points in this story. Have you ever seen or done something heroic? What happened? Write about it.

INFO CENTRE

GLOSSARY

AIR	if you grab air, you perform a jump of some sort
AVALANCHE	large mass of snow, ice and earth that suddenly moves down the side of a mountain
BINDINGS	part of a snowboard to which the boarder's boots connect
FREESTYLE	style of skiing or snowboarding focused on doing tricks
HALFPIPE	U-shaped trench with smooth walls that is used by snowboarders for aerial tricks
JERK	someone who is foolish or mean
SHREDDER	snowboarder, particularly a talented one
SPONSOR	give money and support to someone who is competing in a contest of some kind
SUPERPIPE	larger version of a normal halfpipe. The walls in a superpipe can measure as high as 6 metres (20 feet).

CREATORS

SCOTT CIENCIN › Author

Scott Ciencin is a *New York Times* bestselling author of children's and adult fiction. He has written comic books, trading cards, video games and television shows, as well as many non-fiction projects. He lives in Florida, USA, with his beloved wife, Denise, and his best buddy, Bear, a golden retriever.

ABURTOV › Illustrator

Aburtov is a graphic designer and illustrator who has worked in the comic book industry for more than 11 years. In that time, Aburtov has coloured popular characters such as Wolverine, Iron Man, Punisher and Blade. He recently created his own studio called Graphikslava. Aburtov lives with his beloved wife in Monterrey, Mexico, where he enjoys spending time with family and friends.

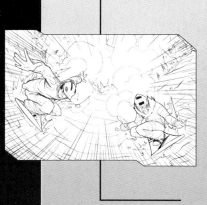

ANDRES ESPARZA › Inker

Andres Esparza has been a graphic designer, colourist and illustrator for many different companies and agencies. Andres now works as a full-time artist for Graphikslava studio in Monterrey, Mexico. In his spare time, Andres loves to play basketball, hang out with family and friends, and listen to good music.

FARES MAESE › Colourist

Fares Maese is a graphic designer and illustrator. He has worked as a colourist for Marvel Comics, and as a concept artist for the card and role-playing games Pathfinder and Warhammer. Fares loves spending time playing video games with his Graphikslava colleagues, and he's an awesome drummer.

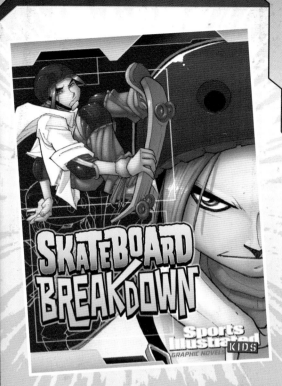
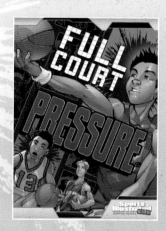

HOT S...
HOT
FORMAT!

Graphic

PAINTBALL PUNK

Sports Illustrated KIDS GRAPHIC NOVELS

BMX BLITZ

Sports Illustrated KIDS GRAPHIC NOVELS

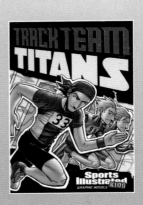

TRACK TEAM TITANS

Sports Illustrated KIDS GRAPHIC NOVELS

FULL COURT FLASH

Sports Illustrated KIDS GRAPHIC NOVELS

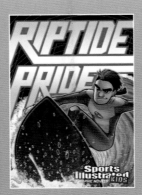

RIPTIDE PRIDE

Sports Illustrated KIDS GRAPHIC NOVELS

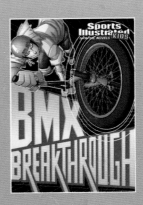

BMX BREAKTHROUGH

Sports Illustrated KIDS GRAPHIC NOVELS

Sports Illustrated KIDS
GRAPHIC NOVELS